MW01612019

Anchoring Words

Anchoring Words

LaVeda R. Bailey

Copyright © 2012 by LaVeda R. Bailey.

| ISBN: | Softcover | 978-1-4691-3449-9 |
| | Ebook | 978-1-4691-3450-5 |

All rights reserved. No part of this book may be reproduced or transmitted in any form or by any means, electronic or mechanical, including photocopying, recording, or by any information storage and retrieval system, without permission in writing from the copyright owner.

This book was printed in the United States of America.

To order additional copies of this book, contact:
Xlibris Corporation
1-888-795-4274
www.Xlibris.com
Orders@Xlibris.com
106862

CONTENTS

KINDREDS

STAND TALL ON YOUR KNEES

BIRTH TIL DEATH

This book is dedicated to

My son, Jeremiah

Acknowledgements

To all the voices I have listened to in a lifetime of reading are the voices of special people, who have cared enough to push me, challenge me, counseled me, and loved me. At the top of that long list of significant friends are:

- My father (heavenly father), who was guiding my path.
- My family and friends who has never stopped encouraging me along the way.
- Maya Angelou who introduced me to the power of pen.
- S. Tyler my teacher who introduce the narrative of poetry eternal truth into concrete realities.
- My grandmother (Othree) saying, "try to, write you, never know somebody might feel you."
- My husband for continual support.

FAMILY

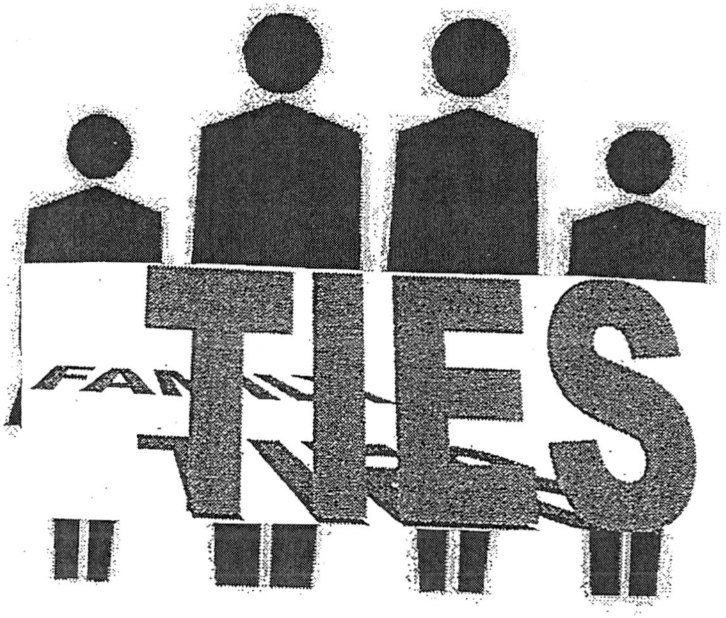

A Family's Day

Hi, there beautiful, what are we eating?
I need you to iron my shirt, for tomorrow's meeting?

Hello, kids how was your day?
Go outside, if you want to holler and play.

I had a bad day and would like to unwind.
Give me peace and quiet, are you will get a peace of my mind.

It's time for my favorite show.
Please be quiet? Are you must go.

I'm running this house; you must go by my rules.
As long as your under my roof, you're going to school.

Do better than I did, if you want to succeed.
I put the dirt down; you're the water and the seed.

I'm harsh and strict for a reason, until you grow.
Coming home one day to a family, you will know.

Whose Dream Is It Really?

The American Dream
A wish, we hope, strive and work hard for it seems.

Now we have the lottery game.
A devils dream seeking pain.

The poor man getting poorer;
And the wealthier making more.

When they advertise superstars with $100 or more tennis shoes.
They don't mention the parents working overtime to make do.

One and a half cars in the yard.
Daddy working extremely hard
Mama praying, "Help us Lord."

A home which needs much repair
Kids don't want to go to school, because they don't care.

Working overtime to save a dime.
Children wondering when do you have time?

Education if you can afford it may not be what it takes.
Higher degrees seem to be filling the place.

A dream can become a nightmare.
Money don't care, it just put you there.

It's up to you, to know what you want to be.
You have the lock, now use the key.

Home Is . . . .

They say home is where the heart is, but where is the heart?

Commonplace things is not a profit, when your family distraught.

To avert the loneliness, children are overdosing all over the world.

The war in Iraq is not the only thing killing our boys and girls.

Home is a place where love is shown.

Home is walls for children to roam.

Home is painted in many colors to soothe all moods.

Home is a place mom cooks our favorite foods.

Home is a place where you can always go.

Home is love, no matter how old you grow.

Why We Are Assembled?

Where join together by only one
Whose kind to all daughters and sons
She's there when were weeping, she's there when we fall
Because she's one mother who assembled us all.

But though no hand goes out her way
A million words go everyday
In the corridor's everywhere
Mother's face flashes through the air.

And if were not happy, if were not well
Mother's touch can surely tell
The little words can cross all space;
But mother is a friend in any place;

Lord, Lord let us fall
How I wonder she stood us all
Up above her angriness so high.
Like a mother in the sky.

And for the little bad rascals, which she say
And showing intelligence and knowledge we pray.

That is why mother and child are assembled this day.

Kids

Have fun
But don't play video's and stay on the computer to long.
Don't be a couch potato
Or a slacker
Or a hater
Go play ball in the field
Jump rope down the block
Complete painting, writings and an essay
And write songs
Use your brain to compose
Don't forget "be all you can be"
Have faith
Think
Travel all you can
Climb to the mountain top
Don't forget the dream.

Before Daddy's Surgery

Dad I love you more than words can say.

A fter today, I'm praying even harder everyday.

D ad you have given me so much through the years.

D eliverance from this, I give you my tears.

Y our grace and mercy will see you through, your son will be Here until Your Anew.

When Are You Going To Finish?

Mama, I don't want to be, what you want me to be.

See God gave me a mind to choose my own destiny.

I'm truly sorry, if you disagree.

But, I believe you should be happy as long as I'm getting my degree.

I didn't bring home any children's, like many of my friends.

You did not have to watch me day and night wondering when I will be in.

I did not drink or use drugs.

Nor did I hang out in the street with thugs.

So, no matter what I chose to do with my life.

Please be happy with my work and strife.

You taught me to be honest and true.

Now, this is my chance to grow up like you.

It may have taken me a little longer to achieve my goal.

But, now I have my degree of choice, I can always hold.

Prevention

Don't give your daughter birth control

Teach her self control

Don't give your son a condom

Give him a confrontation

Give your child a curfew

Not a cell phone to call you when there threw.

Show your child about friendship

Not only courtship

Be proactive

Not inactive

To prevent anything we must sometimes know the danger.

If a child is to stay in a child's place, who do they talk to about strangers?

We send our children into the world without any protection.

Then were angry with teachers and preachers when our kids, return with infections.

Parents, the children are still your baby.

Can they raise a child, or will you have another one maybe?

Sh!!!!!!!!!!!!!!!!!!!!!!!!!!!!!!!!

Don't tell our secret.
I will give you a treat
Know one plays these games in the street.

Maybe it's your daddy, pastor or a friend
He is not suppose to touch you anywhere
Feel on you or touch your skin.

He took you to his house and gave you something to drink.
When you woke up, you did not know what to think.

Your body feels different, you were even sore
He said, he wants to wrestle with you on the floor.

You told him to stop touching you, he showed you porn on TV.
Then you told him to take you home, this is not where I want to be.

He said, SH!!!! About the day, know one can know.
When I got home, I called 911 to his door.

SH!!!!!! Is only a word used for a baby I was told.
I'm a little to old for any grown man to hold.

Are You A Father?

Highest honor God gives you
The seed comes from the man
Blood type of the child is in your hand.
The father gives the child his identity.
Fatherhood is an inherited trait.
A blessing for you to take care of and take.
Discipline and sole provider
Biological father sometimes not around
Surrogate father wears the crown.
Father is the progenitors
Head of the house, not to abuse
Provide leadership, not only dominate, nor used as a check tool.
Abba, has a order to uphold
Take out his baby girl; show her how a man is to take her hand.
Show his son how to be a man.
Donation of a seed to multiply was not God's only reply.
Are you a father? If so, why?

Movie Roots

Starting at The Learning Tree, Stompin at the Savoy
Go Man Go, Baby Boy
Just Chillin, Much Ado About Nothing
Guess Who's Coming To Dinner, Glory
This Club Ain't No Place To Be Somebody
Bad Company in the Color of the Night
Fatal Beauty for Dead Presidents
Disclosure for the Soul of the Game
No Way to Do The Right Thing
Given our Birthright.

It's Your Birthday

Thirty years ago, a new arrival hit the world.

It was a boy! Who became a great black man, not a girl.

He shows great hope for our black American dreams.

His love for our Black History is amazingly seen.

This friend of mind is also a handsome, fine brother.

Within him, I see intelligence, consideration and concern for others.

Now, knowing this friend for a short period, as mind.

I believe like vintage wine, he is getting better with time.

I'm sure your mother, is proud of the birth of her child.

You have fought a great fight, and definitely proud.

This day is yours to be true.

Because there is know one else like you.

See your life is worth celebrating "Today"

Because, tomorrow may never come your way.

And, I wish you the best; and I'm proud to be your friend this day

Just to let you know, Happy Birthday, each and everyday.

Women Struggle Not In Vain

Women suffrage gave me rights
Oppressing them showed me a victorious fight.

Many struggle in pain
Equality for my rights was the gain.

Nineteenth Amendment gave me the right to vote.
Serving all in spite their hopes.

Revolutionary women justified the cause
History of women, affected us all.

Texas Woman's University was the tool I need.
So these women can see their seed.

Black Women's

B lack sisters suffered twice as much.

L iving behind their oppressed man, being Masters, mistress and such.

A fter all this, they stayed strong.

C hisholm, Shirley became our first presidential hope.

K eeping the broken homes, yesterday and now is not a joke.

W omens movement did not fight for Black women rights on a whole.

O k, for Black women to work as a cook for $2.00 a day, I'm told.

M en atonement through the "Million Man March."

E verlasting memories, but only a start.

N evertheless, the Black Women pride and love was always true.

S ee through our double discrimination, God saw us through.

Black Man's Criminal
Court Nightmare

I'm *arrested* and accused
Given *advisement* to use
Next a *preliminary hearing* comes
Pre-Trial conference motions that stunned
Trial takes place
Sentencing for the case
Once it is all said and done
The black man's nightmare begun.

My Nigger

The word we use to say what's up

Not realizing how hard our ancestors fought to break it up.

Nigger is a lazy person: not a person we refer to because of color.

You should not degrade someone because you are hollering at each other.

The use of word is a hateful thing.

Saying nigger is pulling down our culture and shame to our queens and kings.

Learn before you speak.

How do you greet others at home and on the street?

Trim Keeper

One day I met this barber in the parking lot at my car, with this line.

"My shops across the street come by and visit sometime."

He is an entrepreneur, working his shop.

Hollering at all types of people on the block.

I called him on his offer, with my son in mind.

He seem sincerely humble, and one of a kind.

The barber knew Jesus that blew my mind.

He serviced his client with a smile at all times.

They all returned from miles.

To receive his courteous service and his freestyles.

It is good to see our black brothers working hard

Not hustling in the street, on sitting on the porch in the yard.

I'm proud to see our black men trying to succeed.

I admire the trim keepers providing a service we will always need.

Shake That

The earthquake does not shake like this.

Moving your body and shaking your hips.

Men giving tips to a stranger on the stage.

Satisfying lusting desires at any age.

Vibrating on hips while rotating their lips.

Making a grown man flip.

Private room dances for a price.

Drinking and smoking to entice.

Moving thoughts into different places.

Getting wet in all different spaces.

Shake that in the world for major faces.

Strong Sister

DON'T FEEL DETACHED AND ALONE

STRONG SISTER, STAY STRONG

YOU HAVE TAKEN CARE OF OTHERS, BUT HAVE YOU TAKEN CARE OF YOURSELF?

STRONG SISTER, WHO IS LEFT?

TROUBLE DO NOT LAST FOREVER

STRONG SISTER, THINK CLEVER

I AM IMPORTANT TO GOD

STRONG SISTER, THE ONLY MAN WHO IS NOT A FRAUD.

FIND YOUR GIFT.

STRONG SISTER, GIVE EACH OTHER A LIFT

LET YOUR HEALING BEGIN

STRONG SISTER, NEVER ENDS . . . .

A Letter From The Golden Oldies

Gee Whiz, I'm Sittin on (The Dock of the Bay) thinking, I can't Stop
Loving You.
Mighty Love from Mr. Big Stuff doing The Twist and Groove Me.
You have my Soul Man and I'm in a Purple Haze. Ain't No Sunshine
only Lonely Teardrops.
Let's Stay Together, I'll take you there. I Believe In You, Skinny Legs and
All. Only the Strong Survive. I Say a Little Prayer.
LaLa Means I Love You, You Beat Me to the Punch.
There is a Thin Line between Love and Hate. The Twist.
There Goes My Baby Backfield in Motion.

Gold Digger

I can't put too much effort in an unemployed brother.

I can't even handle the brother who asks me to go out, saying, "Do you have me covered."

I'm digging for your wallet you say.

I have my own car, kid and a mortgage to pay.

The above are bills that are always real and here to stay.

The bill comes every month.

So, you just want me to settle with any chump.

Just because I want a man with a plan.

I'm called a gold digger on hand.

I am sure a man wants a woman with more than just ass.

He wants a lady with class.

Oh yea, by the way in order to dig you must have tools.

A little skill, some sense, were not all fools.

Mama told me "that everything that glitters isn't always gold."

If the IRS-take it, car accident paralyze you, what do I have to hold?

Inspiring Things

God all mighty who created us all.
Grandma, saying, "Watch it you will fall."

My teacher who supported my writing
My neighbor from a far, who stop me from fighting.

My mom telling me, I will stand by your side.
My dad struggling at work in the heat and rain to provide.

The 19th Amendment giving me a chance to vote.
A job to go to and fulfill my hopes.

An opportunity to have a choice in life.
Going to any public place without it saying, "Black or Whites."

Waking up to see the bird flocking their wings.
Seeing, walking, talking and hearing are inspiring things.

Black Women In History
Despite The Limitations

Women's History has a lot to do with me.

Without Mary Bethune mark, I would not have a chance to receive a four year accredited college degree.

Mary Mahoney, paved the road for registered nurses, so all mankind could be cared for.

Sojourner Truth oratored lectures against slavery and for women's right.

Harriet Tubman, "Moses of her People" led the fight.

—Itch

I could not exactly write the word.

But men use this word like it is a verb.

It is actually a noun, to disgrace our womanhood.

Not a man's best friend, don't be misunderstood.

In videos, I'm seeing our bodies exposed.

Yet, men are producing them and calling us hoes.

They say, "The media is raising our kids."

But sometimes a woman has to do what she got to do, to pay the bills.

No excuse needed to make a living, yet men enjoy the thrill.

See those female dogs you call them, are others sisters, mothers and cousins that's cold.

Now, do you want the females in your family called—itches and hoes?

Failure Is Not An Option

True Life Story About Inmate
Willie Francis, Electrocuted Twice

They tried to electrocute me, it didn't work.

I killed someone for his watch and wallet with four dollars, in November 1944.

I was a fifteen year old black youth, with a three day trial telling me I will have life no more.

No trial transcript, no change of venue, no motion new trial, no appeal had been filed on the floor.

May 3, 1946, I'm seventeen strapped to the electric chair in a cold corridor.

I lived, despite their glare.

I appealed to the U.S. Supreme Court asking them to forbid the state a second execution attempt in that chair.

I told them, "It's cruel and unusually punishment and they are violating my eight amendment rights."

Supreme Judge Stanley Reed said, "been shocked again isn't cruel", and he won the fight.

May 9, 1946 my coffin was closed with a body that night.

Moving Faster, Going Where?

My ancestors started with their feet.

Then came horses and buggies in the street.

Train and box cars to carry supply.

Airplanes came from the sky.

Trucks on the freeway to carry fleet.

Buses and rail system to move us from our cars off the street.

Gas prices rising everyday.

People wondering how to save for this price of living way.

When I am having a hard time living, trying to pay my lease.

Government can not really adjust this price of living increase.

I'm Telling You What I Know, Not What I Heard

I woke up this morning with activity of my limbs.

Knowing others isn't as fortunate to walk in the park, or go running in the gym.

Life has been like a roll of tape, it is transparent.

And it fixes and heals many things we love and hate.

Watching a kid die slowly from a gunshot wound to the head.

Makes me see bad things for our children's to dread.

Drugs on every corner for sell.

Black on Black crime, climbing the scale.

Mothers, aunts, grandmothers going to funerals every month.

Children are growing up within a single family household and drunks.

Being a female in the world today.

I have to pray for one and all each and everyday.

God believes in me, now I need to believe in the word.

I'm telling you what I know, not what I heard.

KINDREDS

Love People, Use Things

We live today in a cruel world.
Know one tells us about the bad boys and bad girls.
Danger is everywhere, it has no color
There is no such thing as a safe neighborhood my brother.
Today we seem to "love things and use people"
Hum! Money or friends which one are you keeping?
The morals of the world today are sad.
Women and Men are trying to share others love one's, that's bad.
If we can love something or someone that's not ours.
This world truly is going sour.
We need to help all people
And take care of our dreams.
Love People, Use Things.

Between Visits

You say you want a lady
I need a man that is not shady
Don't say your making love
When you leave in a ten-minute interval
I know I'm your friend
Now we are lovers
We can't even pretend
This is a hard task to do
With you knowing me and me knowing you.
Under and over the sheets, we could always talk.
But having these visits are really distraught.
I am not only trying to reach out and touch you every time you come my
way.
See affection is the way I show my love and play. Now don't get it twisted,
I'm attracted to you.
Don't you think by now if I wanted you I know what to do?
Time is what you make of it, don't waste mind
I'm a damn good woman, which is one of a kind
If you look deep you know this is true.
You love me and I love you.

A Gentleman

His touch was soft.
His words are sweet.
A gentle hug, that brings you to your feet.
His kindness overbearing
He is generous and caring
Makes me wonder, who he is marrying
He opens doors
He is also polite
Not very much makes him curse or fight
This man is a single dad
Who understands some problems I had
He worked many long nights, and ask for little
He picked me up when my car was down, and wasn't bitter
He sings in the choir
With a lovely deep voice
He praised the lord at his own choice
Watching this dad, I respect him so
A gentleman, where did they go?

My Best Friend

He's been by my side through the years.
He listens to all my mistakes, and my tears.

He called, when he traveled afar.

He taught me how to drive my car.

He brought music to my ear that taught me love.
He believes in my love up above.

He cherished my thoughts and beliefs.

He supported me when I was going through grief.

He taught me the hardest lesson, don't fall for everything.
Then my best friend gave me a ring.

Perpetuity

Like a circle

In the sky

Like a diamond in the ruff

Like the sound of music in your car

Like your children's love, no matter where you are

Like time on a clock, goes around

Like death stigma, brings a frown

Like love—portion of time.

They Got Half the Money and All the Lovin

They are moving up the corporate ladder.

Not only cooking at home with all the batter.

They take care of the office and the home.

Doing all this while making beds and scheduling appointments on the phone.

Some call them mommy, some call them boss.

In either position they pay the cost.

The honey he gave us to help us play.

Standing or lying she makes our day.

They got half the money and all the lovin all the time.

I am happy they are each one of a kind.

What A Friend

I woke up to a phone call by a friend.
She said, "she needed my man to pick her up again."

You know after the second time, my mind wonder about these calls.

She constantly asked, "When I was getting married? Not knowing my man children's she was carrying.

I baby-sit, my soon to be stepchild in my house. Took this so called friend to the doctor for advice.

I bought her children clothes for birthdays and such.
Not knowing I was going to bed every night with their daddy's touch.

With friends like these, it's unfair.
Because there are true friends out there, that cares.

My advice, to have a friend
You must be one, until the end.

I was not raised to hate others, when they hurt you.
Just ask God for strength to see you through.

If life don't teach you about being a friend. Remember you have one within.

Everyone have feelings, some good, and some bad.
See there are others out there who always want what you have.

Just a reminder when you hurt someone,
It has a boomerang effect.
The choices of friends are like the rainbow of colors, and you can select.

The Air Of Love

You can smoke it without a light.
(Love lights every second)

You don't have any ashes.
(Love blows it away)

It is not bad for your health.
(Love gives you support)

It aid in your living longer.
(Aids your heart)

This air makes you stronger.
(You can breathe it everyday)

The Affair

She showed me an artificial love
My woman hugs and kisses was not from above
Her affair with another man tore me apart
But I'm thanking God, for my loving heart.
My child was placed in the middle of this mess
I'm thankful for my son, because I'm blessed
I am going to be a father, not only a dad
Because of my parent's upbringing, I can do this even if I'm mad
My woman unfaithfulness shattered my trust
But my strong will is truly a must.
My mother taught me God is real
No matter how much the devil steals.
When we talk about the word, I'm happy to know.
What I'm learning is helping me grow.
Daddy said, "Getting even won't solve the solution."
I'm seeing slowing, the resolution.
Gaining knowledge increases my sorrow.
My woman action, can't steal my tomorrow.

Special Delivery

YOU SAY YOU'RE IN NEED

AND YOU ORDER SOMETHING REAL

SOMETHING YOU CAN TOUCH AND SOMETHING YOU CAN FEEL.

YOU ORDER SOMETHING LONG AND HARD.

ECTASY IS YOUR CHARGE

NO BATTERIES NEEDED

SATISFACTION TO PLEASE

IT DOES COME WITH A MONEY BACK GUARANTEE.

SO PLEASE SIGN FOR YOUR ORDER

ENJOY YOUR SPECIAL DELIVERY FLIGHT

BUCKLE UP

IT IS GOING TO TAKE ALL NIGHT.

What You See

Do not feel bad because you are alone.
Count you blessings; take care of your home.
Lack of intimacy sometimes is a plus.
Because what I am seeing in this world is a disgust.
People walking hand to hand, but not heart to heart.
Lying with each other, but really apart.
The person sitting in the front seat is not always on the front line.
Hoping and dreaming for a family to find.
What you see in life, is not always what you get.
The divorce rate of America show's this with much regret. They say,
The main reason for divorce is money.
You had money before marriage, isn't that funny?
Then you say, I found out my lover was cheating and/or bi-sexual, what
do I do?
Ask God to deliver you.
Do not say, "I am staying for my kids."
God is not the author of confusion, for what they did.
What you see, may cause you to go blind.
Close your eyes and pray sometimes.

You Know The Man

Hi, there, "I'm Romeo."
What's your name?
My name is Lovely.
That is a nice name for a lovely fine lady.
Yea, but it would be even lovelier if you'll go away.
So I can have some peace and quiet today.
Baby, I can offer you the world.
I can make you feel like a woman not a girl.
I can give you something no man can touch.
I can make you scream and holler and such.
Okay brother, I'm listening to your rap
But, you fail to see who told you, your all that. First, I didn't ask for the
world, maybe just peace.
If your treat me with a little respect, I might listen to your speech.
Second, I'm already a woman not a girl.
Last I check, only my man rocks my world.
And for all the noises and such.
Like Hammer said, "You can't touch."
See a man is not only judged by his size.
And a woman is not always trying to capitalize. Maybe if you had an
approach with substance in hand.
Maybe,
You Know the Man.

Tune Ups

You are just an average lady.

You will do until something better comes along.

You are alright, but you are not my baby at home.

You're cool as my part time lover. Other women, back burner flame

Side lady under the cover, but you can not bear my last name.

My spare, due to that time of the month.

My back up girl with a lot under her trunk.

Standby when I need a weekend fix.

Outside woman for kicks.

When I am in need of much repair.

I just call and make an appointment for my spare.

It Ain't Mines

The first words after conception these days

I think the woman should reply, "It's not"

Gentlemen think before you holler.

This is a lifetime commitment not just for a dollar

A boy or girl needs their parents

Don't fuss about who is at fault, take the gift to heart.

It ain't mines, should never be in your thoughts.

Technically, it ain't yours; it's a gift from God that was bought.

It ain't mines is a horrible claim

Remember that seed, bears your blood and name.

What Are You Looking For?

Why do brothers play these silly games?
Don't they realize all the hurt and pain?

I wonder if mom really knows about her son.
The many loves, he brought home, but now there is none.

A man always says, "I'm the man."
How can you believe that having only one-night stands?

If you are a real man, you can handle a relationship.
Not just hanging with your friends saying, "I've slept with another _itch."

Some men believe if they feed you, that you owe them something.
I think the man should be happy to have you in his company.

See the house, cars, are nice things,
But how much happiness can it bring?

Believe it or not money runs out.
Now tell me brother what do you got?

If you base your relationship on material things.
Ask yourself what does that mean?

If baby got back
And brother's all that
Remember looks fade, like age, then your trap.

See a one way street sometimes come to a dead end.
Do you want a part-time lover or a full-time friend?

Deadly Tongue

WHAT YOUR HEART BEAT

YOUR MOUTH SPEAK

THINK BEFORE YOU UTTER WORDS

BRIDLE YOUR TONGUE

BECAUSE ONCE YOU SPEAK,

IT IS ALREADY DONE.

Ain't Scared

You said, "You did not want kids."
Then you came into my life
Now you have a son and a wife
Being the man that you are
We became a family from near and far
My son calls you dad
And I call you honey
You are still a real cat
I will bet all my money
You walked in the door
Single and real
A man with a sincere heart and not just appeal
Though I'm your girl
And he is your little guy
Your still real cool and dress real fly.
Handling being a stepfather is a task to forever hold.
Being a man, spirit, body and soul.
You treat us as one
Though the job was not yours
You took it anyway
Knowing there might be trouble any day.
I'm thankful for a man who can lead his family today and saying,
"Ain't Scared what others might say."

Dream Maker or Dream Breaker

My love cost me more than I can afford.
Every lover I thought I had, brought a different dream aboard.
It not only cost me money but a lots of gleam.
I planned my dreams with my lover, but he chose other things.
Dream breaker, call Satan had to do his job to.
So the maker can be the breaker of a dream come true.
They say follow your heart.
I say follow God.
Because a man steps are ordered, even against the odds.

Different Drivers

(Sometimes God Replaces the Driver for Many Reasons)
They were there only for a season
Loves comes and go for many reasons.
It could be the wrong woman or man.
You need to re-evaluate your plan.
Might be in the wrong place.
Maybe they have a different taste.
Sometimes your not equally yoke.
Don't drive with insurance hope.
The bible said, "When a man findeth a wife, he findeth a good thing."
Sometimes new/used vehicles are down payment for that Queen or King.

Ready Made

Not many choices from women today
Some have children and one on the way
The choice is still mine to choose my mate.
God told me to multiply not just make mistakes.
I know a child is a gift, nothing wrong from God.
I'm just not ready for a ready made family to solve.
I pray to follow the proper steps in order.
Get a job, house, wife and then a son or daughter.
I'm not trying to discriminate on anyone.
But, I am a single man that enjoys his fun.
My life isn't based on nine months and it's done.
I believe I should "have it my way" and be a father to my son.
If it is already done, I will take what is ready.
But, in the meantime I would love to go steady.
Ready made with many additives.
Family made with a narrative.

Peace Out

Holler if you hear me
Call me if you are near me
Boo, I'm missing you
The late night talks and your smile to
You can complete my thoughts
I miss our walks
E-mail when you can
Drive by and hold my hand
We can listen to jazz on the radio
Sit outside on the porch and watch the people show
Hit me on my cell during the day
I will be driving about and call you back on the expressway.
Peace Out

What Do I Get In Return?

We made a promise to stick like glue.
No matter what goes down, or what we do.
I'll help you through college with emotional support.
When I got the news your were pregnant, I was not ready for that report.
Oh well, I'll be traveling again to do what I do.
I always keep in touch through and through.
You were my friend when I started with a little success.
Now you my buddy when I bling-bling my boat, house and cars because
I am truly blessed.
I regret to tell you someone else have my heart.
The key to my house and my family start.
You can not have anymore children, which mean you can not have me.
I am sorry to end this love affair with sa Ia ye.

A Real Man

A Real Man
Says what he means
And means what he says
He can build you up in any kind of way.
He can lift your spirit and free your mind.
He knows what to say, and how to find . . .
He can take your body and blow your mind.
A Real Man is one of a kind.

Attack Of The Heart

In your house we creep
In love we sleep
When your woman left town
Lots of things went down
Your love was misleading
And your heart was deceiving
Now I am left with a heart grieving
It was my fault to declare you time
Giving you what you want at a drop of a dime
I expect what I got
And I got what is not
A heart beat stopped by a blood clot.

Baby, "I Love You"

Saying I love you, cost you your life
Seek and find a husband or wife
Always looking for a bride or groom
Not knowing who is real or who is going to bring you gloom
The three letter word made to find your match.
Another person saying what you want to hear, to get their catch.
If you can respect me, love will grow
You must know who you are, not only what I know
Love is compromising, when you know you are wrong
Picking up the phone, when you are late coming home.
Show me respect, I will give you love.
Better than what dreams are made of.

Living Single

What is singleness?
To be separate, unique and whole.
Because in the book of Genesis,
God made someone else as a compatible companion, I'm told
I'm sorry to say,
But marriage does not make your loneliness go away.
God gave us a right to choose our mate.
It is our decision, about whom to date.
Do not fall in love with someone who says "I need you"
Because God said, "He would supply all your needs, to see you through."
Remember, we are just like keys on a janitor key ring.
All separate and unique, but we fit only one thing.
God did not make us all alike
We have different fingerprints
Remember even the first parents of this earth was not so content.
Adam said, "God I was fine with my animals until you sent Eve, What's
up? Adam had to adapt to change, open his doors and have trust.
I know we have all been hurt before.
But we also have been dirty even more.
Every time we are dirty, we take a bath.
Every time we hurt, we might cry.
So just remember to keep our faith with the man in the sky.
Remember everyone was not born to be married
Think about the birth of Jesus and how he was carried.
In him you are complete.
Single, whole and unique.

Strength

The strength of my life is the lord
He said my salvation will be thy reward.
As we know anyone can go downstream without a paddle
Now a Christian journey is an upstream battle.
See our strength cometh against principalities
But our troubles, usually brings us to reality.
For by strength shall no man prevail?
Because Gods love will always avail
Strength can come only when we apply the power.
Even though we don't know it, we have the power every second,
and every hour.

Going Down

Now I lay me down to sleep
Who are you asking, for your soul to keep?
Are you bending down to ask for something again?
Don't you think Gods love is within?
God knows your troubles before you bow down.
So don't say, "Here I am again" with a frown.
He said, "Lo I'll be with you always" each day
Get closer to him and pray.
Worship him honestly, by going down
Don't be afraid to make a sound.
Trouble and God will always be around.
One is going to stay and stand on solid ground.
Your approach makes the different for all your results.
Are you faking, lying, are hoping for spiritual guts?
If you don't want to get your knees dirty when you pray.
Hope, Joy, Love and Peace comes with going down this way.

My Man

There is one man, who is good to me,
He said, no matter where you are I will be.
I am your best friend until the end of time;
I can look at any situation, and see my friend.
He said, "He will stand by my side until the end".
I can call my man anytime.
See there is no answering machine or busy signal on his line
He is my best friend, with all power;
See he will never have to buy my love with candy of flowers.
I can sit down and talk to him about anything.
My man said, "Never be afraid to give or bring."
Last, but not least, Jesus gives me love
Better than anyone, could hope for or dream of.

Mama, Where Does Sickness Come From?

Mama, where does sickness come from?
My child only the devil.
So, why does, God let him make me ill?
It is not his will that is why he made pills.
See healing baby, is for everyone.'
But the devil comes to devour our fun.
It is written, "Whatever you believe when you pray you will have them".
You can chose to keep your sickness are believe in him.
When you are sick, call on the Lord name to save your soul
Because, "all things work together for good to them that love
God."
Don't let the devil take hold.
"Nothing shall by any means hurt you"
Sickness doesn't discriminate, nor glorify his truth.
Sickness will keep you hostage, if you don't have faith.
So only talk about healing, not what your feeling when you pray.

The Mind

The devil attacks our five senses.
Because he knows it is our largest expense.

What type of mind will you have when he attacks?
It does not matter if you white or black.

Will you have a reprobate mind?
Refuse to get knowledge of God.
Are stay forever wondering is this all a fraud?

You can choose to have an empty mind.
Nothing there until you fill it with something you find.
Or even worse, with the devils kind.

Then there is the fleshly mind.
Let no man beguile you worshiping angel stranger.
Because life will offer you continuous danger.

Beware of the defiled mind.
See's nothing as pure.
Will soon have plenty of things in life to fear.

Maybe you will wonder like the carnal mind.
Doubting all mankind.
Wanting to have all man possessions, but running out of time.

Or could you be a man who can't sleep for an unrelaxed mind?
Needing to shield himself with the helmet of salvation.
And return to his master to fill up at the Jesus station.

Warranty VS. Guarantee

When life breaks down,
What do you want?
Life gives you a warranty, when it gets broke.
You can replace it with hope.
God is a guarantee, it will never get broke.

Don't Give Up

Why bother to fight?
See tomorrow is just another night.

You can't run from the devil forever.
You must submit to God whenever.

All you have to do when your friends talk about you.
First, know they are not your friends.
But know, there soul can be comprehend.

Second, you can say, "I rebuke you devil."
You're mean, evil, hateful and even clever.

Third, I have a choice to fight or to submit.
Now that I now you will never quit.

But we "wrestle not against flesh and blood."
Not realizing our father already has on the golden glove.

Being a Christian is hard.
Because once one fights over, another enters the yard.

Were placed in a choke hold that is tight.
The "word", is the bell to save our life.

See the devil wears nice designs, He has clothes, cars, money,
friendship and the brother is even fine.
But, don't let him destroy your mind.

Turn it over.
Be a chump, coward, and bend down and pray on those traps.
Don't give up, Gods got your back

Some Are So Heavenly Bound
They're No Earthly Good

Girl, we have the best choir in town.
They can sing like mockingbirds.
But, do they come in with a smile or a frown?

I'm on usher board number four.
We can't be beat in our hand styles.
But, have they ever directed anyone to heaven's door?

Sister Black taught us the "Lord Prayer"
She knows how to pray so well.
But, have she ever witnessed anywhere?

Deacon Green stay on his knees praying so much
I'm not sure why, he ask his name over and over again
But, does he know his son argues with teachers and cuss?

What a Fellowship.
We have in Jesus
Or, are we really on a trip?

So heavenly bound
We have forgotten our Jesus Pass, stating
"Only what we do for Christ will last".

You Messed Up, But You Are Not A Mess

Don't runaway my child.
Stay here and listen for awhile.

Drugs are calling you to the street.
Just say no and be a creep.

Please don't sell your body to survive.
I will work two jobs to keep us alive.

I understand your having a child.
This is a job you will have for a while.

You have to stand strong on your feet.
Go to school every day, don't just sleep.

Now you have an additional mouth to feed.
A baby has to have love, food and needs.

So daddy is a married man.
You were taken advantage of from a one night stand.

He said, "He will pay for an abortion."
But he did not feel the baby kicking in motion.

This is a part of you, no matter what.
Maybe you're not his lady, but you are not a slut.

All have sinned and fallen short.
But seek ye first, for a new start.

I'm glad I have a God to stand and say
You messed up, but you are not a Mess
Hold on and Pray.

If You Were Called, Where Were You Sent?

Jesus said, "My sheep hear my voice, and I know them,
and they follow me."

All men at times fail; now where will you be?

Act on the word you were taught.
Don't forget you must review the bible to walk the walk.

You can not lead anyone talking about inabilities
Because God provided your soul only capabilities.

Being called is definitely a great gift.
But to talk of doubt and unbelief should be a myth.

God has the bomb.
But you have the fuse.
The calling is your choice to use.

The doors only open if you turn the knob.
God will give you the position, if you take the job.

Now you have a position, that's not easy to lead.
Will your flock be destroyed by the lack of knowledge it needs?

Preserve the Fruit

You can lose the tree (divorce), but still preserve the fruit (child).

Train up you fruit to handle dispute.

Labor pains from the fruit will last a lifetime.

Teach the fruit to grow close to God and have faith in mind.

God has a purpose to prevail his pursuit

Grace will preserve at the root.

Your seal makes each fruit unique.

Give them the bible to find and seek.

Parents you must preserve your fruit while they are young.

Don't let bugs like sex, drugs and negative peers, kill your fruit fun.

Keep them around positive Holy Spirit repellant, as much as you can.

Put your fruit in God's hand.

Jehovah's

Jehovah Shammah there when I think I'm alone,

Jehovah Shalom gives me peace in my home

Jehovah Jireh provides me with my all

Jehovah Nissi my victor, never lets me fall

Jehovah Rapha heals my body aches

Jehovah Tsi Kenu, "Lord our Righteous",
to help us survive each fight.

Jehovah protects us through the night.

Delivery

Delivery means to disperse or let go of something.

After your child comes out, it makes you wander

Pain is "But a moment, Ok, hours of Labor"

Raising that child is not only up to a village or a neighbor.

Giving your child away to the street is delivering them a prize.

You will never see again, the pain in their eyes.

A child is delivered to you as a gift.

There is a guarantee on them if you just give them a lift.

This Soulful Body

Don't do with your soul,
What you do with your body.
Dress it up.

See you can't please everyone.
So please your father.
He is your provider, even when others don't want to be bothered.

If you decide to accessorize.
Carry your purse of peace, no matter what size.
Wear your shoes to step out on faith to provide.

Necklace to keep your cross in place.
Remembering Christ on this soulful body for God sake.

Many wear rings to honor each other
Why wear a symbol if the vow is not to your lover.

Christ died for us between two sinners.
Please reminder he sacrificed for our soulful body to be winners.

Faith

Love is the motivator
Faith is the activator

Faith requires time to grow
It's not only who you are, but also whom you know.

If you believe you're going to get a paycheck each week, you're using this.

Faith for something not yet seen, but you expect your job not to forget.

Your money was something you hope for, but the evidence was not yet seen.

James states, "Faith without work is dead".
I know you can't see it, but it is in your future ahead.

Faith is action
Reacting instead of responding is a choice
You are authorized to exercise your voice.

God blessings may come from the bosom of man
So be kind to all, who has sinned.

Sinners believe in the wrong thing, but they believe

Don't criticize your brother; remember you don't know who holds that blessed deed.

Faith never makes sense
So don't question it, just be convinced

Why when it comes to God we need proof?
Believe in Faith, and let it loose.

Days Like This
(Cancer Pains)

It is important not to give up
Keep praying for positive results
Take your fear in a new direction
Your white blood cells can fight this infection.

All attitudes are important
Every minute counts
Medicine, fever, and eating are on going battles to mount.
Chemotherapy happens as a mean to an end.
Don't cry remember your faith within.

When you look into the mirror and see your hair falling out.
Keep praying, don't have doubts
Remember life has twists
Sometimes you might have "days like this".

Fear

False prophets around me daily

Evidence not proven

Appearing untrue

Real things

Bouquet Of Spring Flowers

I began on a semi-journey;
In half of an hour
Later I saw a light which made me see:
Next thing I knew I was a bouquet of spring flowers.
I was surrounded by my friends
Nature was my closest kin.
For some bizarre reason he got angry.
So, then I wonder, and found a stranger.
He offered me, "life or death?"
In my ramification, I chose death, in the end
Why my friend? He asked,
Because, I know nature will come back to comprehend.

Water

Water is a peaceful thing.

It also helps keep you clean.

It is blue and clear in certain places.

It's used even to drink (clean or dirty) in certain nations.

Animals live in this cold or hot environment.

Fish and mammals are so content.

Sometimes water can be very harmful, if you can't swim.

Water is even dangerous when you jump in.

So like other things in life, watch things taking place.

Water can be tranquil or unsafe.

Seedless Chlild

A gift from God, not an accident.
Because the drivers of this vehicle both gave consent.
We always want to blame others for our mistakes.
Yet, we lay and make the choices we make.
My child was born, also to my surprise.
It was the longest nine months, I had to survive.
You said, "You couldn't go to any doctor's appointments",
Because you did not have time.
I'm trying to work to pay for what's mine.
You say, "I tried to give support, but others say it may not be mine."
Because, I only known you for a short period of time.
The question, I asked "are you trying to trap me to stay around?"
Well, I know when you make an adult decision.
It's time to make adult previsions.
Money does not raise a child, it gives support.
Late night changes, bottle making and little sleep, is only just a little effort put forth.
Be a man and raise your child.
From birth to death, he will be here a while.
It may not be a position you were ready to hold.
Your blessing is a blessing that can not be sold.
A role model is important to a girl or boy.
Do they have to choose one from T.V. or a toy?
Today's man wants to lead.
I am giving you the opportunity to water your seed.

The Price We Pay to Lay

This is the pain I feel.
On today with pills.
Years of trust and love.
Wounded without a glove.

I will feel it until the grave.
My sickness would not behave.
Better to love and lost.
Than living, wounded at all cost.

STD's was the thing I caught
A price I never thought
Death was the road taken
Just because of the choices I was making.

I Leave

To my children, I leave my love.
I want you to know, I'm with God up above.
Give your tears, to your children, you are my fruits.
Teach your little ones about ours roots.
Gods makes no mistakes, so don't ask why.
If you think I'm gone look towards the sky.
Granny has walked this earth for eighty-two years.
To see my grandchildren, brought me tears.
I lived longer than what many doctor's said.
Now, I'm walking without my walker, through the shadow of death.
I leave you my smile, and my last breath.
For many great friends, I dwell in a different home.
My new address is heaven, with my green pastures to roam.
For my family, "my yoke is easy and my burdens are light."
So please, everyone bow down tonight.
As I lay here, in my purple dress.
I want you all to know, I'm blessed.
We have had many good times, and you will have many more.
Appreciate what God has enstore.
Your heavenly father will always be there.
Smile with me, this cross we bear.
My children, I leave
Hope, Joy, and Happiness, not despair.

Respect

Pay your respect like you pay your bills, on time.

Love your family before interest becomes fines.

If respect is not paid in time your bill will be past due.

Their spirit will be the collector calling you.

Saying, "I just wanted to let you know you're delinquent"

My body is six feet under and heaven sent.

You did not pay your respect on the day, I went.

Time for Life

If you have ever been locked up, you feel my pain.

Wanting to live, but only seeing the rain.

The bars are cold, night and day.

Food not a homemade gourmet.

Waking up on their time clock.

Not seeing my family, but hearing the lock.

A schedule you never been on before.

Lights off and on can be a bore.

A turn around, they call a cell.

Hoping and praying for bail.

Commissary a dream if your family got some money.

But, let my girl tell it "I don't think so honey."

So now you're a smoker with no cigarettes.

Making deals with much regrets.

Waiting on my trial day.

So I can get out and start my life again, I pray.

I'm Still Here

Cancer did not catch me
Death on the operating table did not hold me
Heart disease did not beat me
Car crash did not defeat me.

The healer spoke to Hezekiah just for me.
Young lady you cannot have children, because conception will kill
thee
My son, Jeremiah and I are here to delivery this message to you.
No matter what you do . . .

No weapon form, will prosper
The power was in my tongue
Before having my child, I lost a daughter and a son
I'm here for a purpose, by his grace.
Walking this earth to eventually one day see his face.

The Clock of Death

I woke up in the middle of the night.
Seeing strange things from left to right.
I tried to scream, but there was no sound.
So I jumped up out of bed, ripping my night gown.
With one arm torn,
I reached for the phone
Not even realizing it was gone.
I ran to the door, screaming and hollering, but all I found was a dollar.
I tried to pick it up, but it would not move.
It just pointed in a direction behind the stool.
So I went to the stool and moved it aside.
At first, all I heard was tick-tock
Then as I looked more, more I found a clock.
Later, while watching the clock,
It struck noon and all I knew, I was back in the room.
My mother came in and I described it to her
She said, it sounded like the clock of death.
I looked for that clock for days in my room:
I looked till I was out of breathe
Later that day I found the clock
And I stood in a state of shock. Not knowing when it would stop.

Quote: "Life ticks like a clock, because you will never know when it's going to stop."

My Global Mind

THANK YOU JESUS FOR KEEPING ME IN MY RIGHT MIND
TODAY.
I ALWAYS WONDER WHAT THE OLD PEOPLE WERE TRYING
TO SAY.
BUT WE ARE BLESSED TO KNOW OTHERS AROUND US.
PAY OUR BILLS WE COMPLAIN ABOUT, AND CATCH A BUS.
SOME PEOPLE HAVE FORGOTTEN WHO THEY ARE.
UNFOURNATELY THEY CAN'T ALWAYS FIND THE KEYS TO
THEIR CAR.
THIS IS NOT A CLINCHE, UNDERSTANDING THINGS IN
CONTEXT.
IT IS REALITY NOWDAYS, REMEMBERING FACES NOT NAMES
AND POETRY TEXT.
YOUNG OR OLD IT DOES NOT DISCRIMINATE.
THE RIGHT SIDE OF YOUR BRAIN HELPS YOUR GLOBAL
MEMORY TO
OPERATE.

Overtime With A Painful Game

(From the death of a Plano basketball player name
    Steve Higginbotham. Died while playing.)

The place was in Lewisville.
Where everyone paid the bill.
To watch the players play.
In which time prevail a sour day.
A young man played a game.
In which no one wants to play the same.
His time was with little despair.
Not knowing everyone cared.
Higg was a friend to all.
Supporting his team when that time call.
Talk no more so very proudly.
Yet his game was won very loudly.
He died in a silent peace.
This made the game consider least.
Higg heart stops pumping on aim.
Therefore, overtime ended with a painful game.

Flowers of the Hour

One shade of light, one day of cold
With one-man grace, I only grow old:
Once planted in a house of eloquent
I wanted more love, but less resent
An hour pass, nevertheless,
But something told me I was bless
Later after an hour
Someone watered me and I became a flower
I was so happy leaving the suppressed ground
But later, I look up and then I frowned
I wish the world could see this hour
The time when God develop the flower
So everyone could stop hating each other
There will be a time in life when we are all going to need that watery
brother.

CPSIA information can be obtained at www.ICGtesting.com
Printed in the USA
LVOW08s0015280514

387530LV00002B/91/P